Diwali

Denise M. Jordan

Heinemann Library

Chicago, Illinois

© 2002 Reed Educational & Professional Publishing
Published by Heinemann Library,
an imprint of Reed Educational & Professional Publishing,
Chicago, Illinois

Customer Service 888-454-2279
Visit our website at www.heinemannlibrary.com

Designed by Sue Emerson, Heinemann Library; Page layout by Ginkgo Creative, Inc.
Printed and bound in the U.S.A. by Lake Book

06 05 04 03 02
10 9 8 7 6 5 4 3 2 1

Library of Congress Cataloging-in-Publication Data
Jordan, Denise M.
   Diwali / Denise Jordan.
      p. cm. — (Candle time)
Includes index.
Summary: A simple introduction to the customs and traditions connected with the Hindu celebration of Diwali.
   ISBN: 1-58810-527-X (HC), ISBN 1-58810-736-1 (Pbk.)
   1. Divali—Juvenile literature. [1. Divali. 2. Fasts and feasts—Hinduism. 3. Hinduism—Customs and practices.
4. Holidays.] I. Title. II. Series.
BL1239.82.D58 J67 2001
294.5'36—dc21
                              2001004629

Acknowledgments
The author and publishers are grateful to the following for permission to reproduce copyright material:
pp. 4, 13 Dinodia/Omni Photos Communications; p. 5 Arvind Garg/Corbis; p. 6 AFP/Corbis; p. 7 Dinodia; p. 8 Joseph Sohm; ChromoSohm Inc./Corbis; pp. 9, 11 Stock Transparency Services Images; p. 10 D. Banerjeb/Dinodia Picture Agency; pp. 12, 14, 20 Trip/H Rogers; p. 15 Robert Lifson; p. 16 Rudi Von Briel/Photo Edit, Inc; p. 17 Catherine Karnow/Corbis; p. 18 Earl & Nazima Kowall/Corbis; p. 19 Ranjit Sen/Dinodia Photo Library; pp. 21, 22 Abir Abdullah/Drik

Cover photograph courtesy of Dinodia/Omni Photos Communications

Every effort has been made to contact copyright holders of any material reproduced in this book. Any omissions will be rectified in subsequent printings if notice is given to the publisher.

Special thanks to our advisory panel for their help in the preparation of this book:

Eileen Day, Preschool Teacher
Chicago, IL

Paula Fischer, K–1 Teacher
Indianapolis, IN

Sandra Gilbert,
Library Media Specialist
Houston, TX

Angela Leeper,
Educational Consultant
North Carolina Department
of Public Instruction
Raleigh, NC

Pam McDonald, Reading Teacher
Winter Springs, FL

Melinda Murphy,
Library Media Specialist
Houston, TX

Helen Rosenberg, MLS
Chicago, IL

Anna Marie Varakin, Reading Instructor
Western Maryland College

Special thanks to R. S. Rajan of the Indo-American Center in Chicago, Illinois, and Smita Parida for their help in the preparation of this book.

Some words are shown in bold, **like this.**
You can find them in the picture glossary on page 23.
You say dih-WALL-ee.

Contents

What Is Diwali?

Diwali is a candle time.

It is a celebration for Hindu people all over the world.

On Diwali, Hindu people celebrate the new year.

When Do People Celebrate Diwali?

People celebrate Diwali in the fall.

It is in October or November.

Diwali can be one or more days long.

What Do People Do During Diwali?

People clean their houses to get ready for Diwali.

They have fairs and dance in the streets.

Family and friends get together.

They share food and tell stories.

What Lights Are There During Diwali?

Diwali means "row of lights."

Oil lamps called **diyas** shine from homes.

People put strings of lights around their houses.

Fireworks light up the night.

What Do Diwali Decorations Look Like?

Many people place a **toran** over their front door.

A toran is made from flowers or cloth.

In some places, women and children draw on the sidewalks.

The drawings are called **rangoli.**

What Foods Do People Eat During Diwali?

Milk is a special food for Hindu people.

During Diwali, people eat sweets made from milk.

| barfi | ladoo | cham cham |

Children eat sweets like **barfi**, **ladoos**, and **cham chams**.

How Do People Dress for Diwali?

sari

Women and girls wear new **saris.**

A sari is a cloth wrapped around the body.

kurta

Men and boys wear new **kurtas.**

A kurta is a long, loose shirt.

What Do Children Do During Diwali?

Some children light **sparklers.**

Children may also give plays or act out skits.

Are There Gifts for Diwali?

Diwali cards may come in the mail.

Some people send money for gifts.

Diwali is a special time for giving.

Quiz

Here are some things you see during Diwali.

Can you name them?

Look for the answers on page 24.

?   ?

Picture Glossary

barfi
(BAR-fee)
page 15

rangoli
(ran-GO-lee)
page 13

cham cham
page 15

sari
(SAH-ree)
page 16

diya
(DEE-yah)
page 10

sparkler
page 18

kurta
(KOOR-ta)
page 17

toran
(tor-AHN)
page 12

ladoo
page 15

Note to Parents and Teachers

Reading for information is an important part of a child's literacy development. Learning begins with a question about something. Help children think of themselves as investigators and researchers by encouraging their questions about the world around them. Each chapter in this book begins with a question. Read the question together. Look at the pictures. Talk about what you think the answer might be. Then read the text to find out if your predictions were correct. Think of other questions you could ask about the topic, and discuss where you might find the answers. Assist children in using the picture glossary and the index to practice new vocabulary and research skills.

Index

Answers to quiz on page 22

diya   sari